AF270609

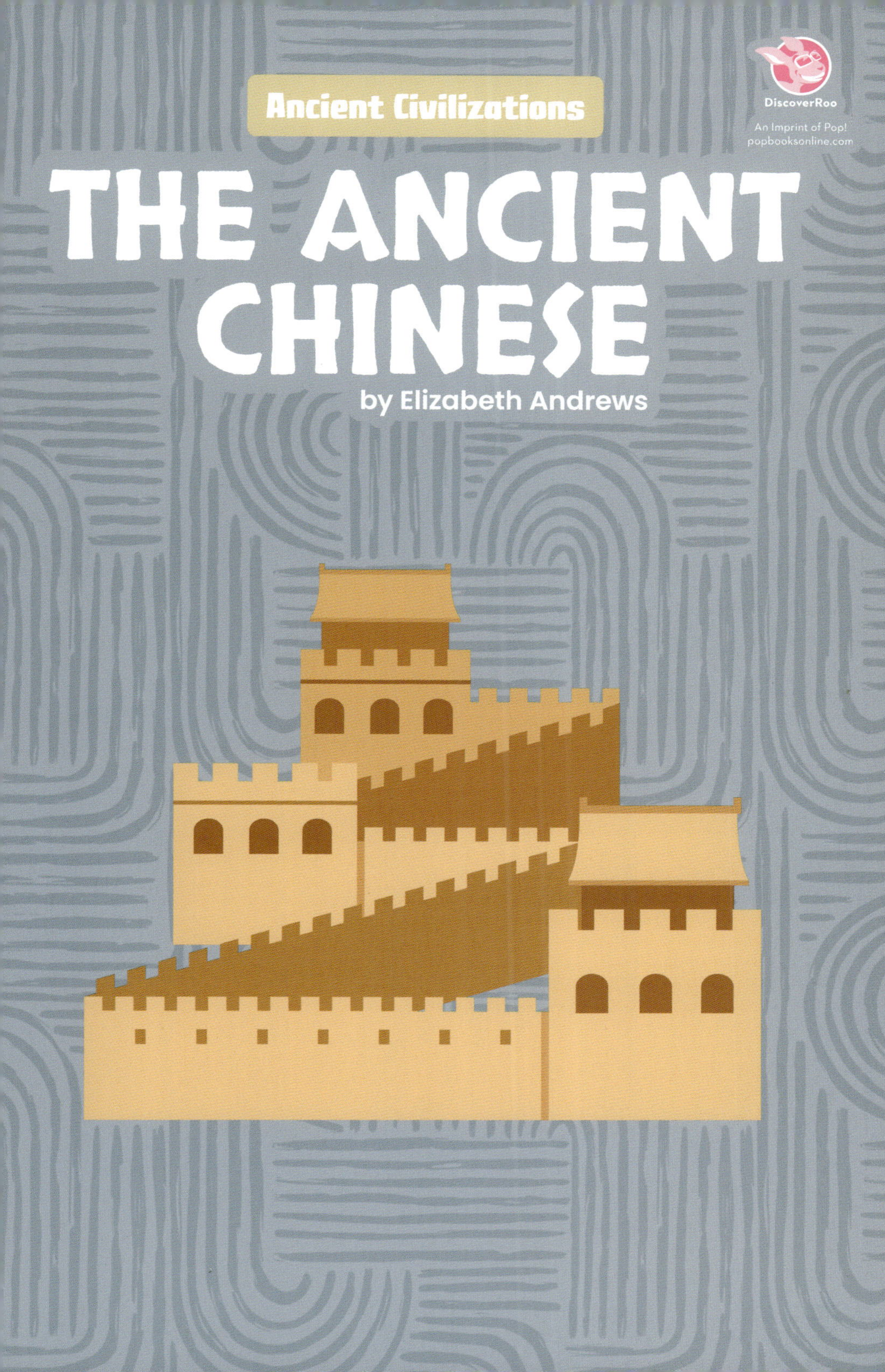

THE ANCIENT CHINESE

by Elizabeth Andrews

popbooksonline.com/anc-chinese

abdobooks.com

Published by Pop!, a division of ABDO, PO Box 398166, Minneapolis, Minnesota 55439. Copyright © 2023 by Abdo Consulting Group, Inc. International copyrights reserved in all countries. No part of this book may be reproduced in any form without written permission from the publisher. DiscoverRoo™ is a trademark and logo of Pop!.

Printed in the United States of America, North Mankato, Minnesota.
102022
012023

THIS BOOK CONTAINS
RECYCLED MATERIALS

Cover Photo: Pictures from History/Getty Images, Shutterstock Images
Interior Photos: Shutterstock Images, Royal Academy of Arts London, The Art Archive/Shutterstock, Historia/Shutterstock, Christopher Pillitz/Getty Images
Editor: Emily Dreher
Series Designer: Laura Graphenteen

Library of Congress Control Number: 2022941120

Publisher's Cataloging-in-Publication Data
Names: Andrews, Elizabeth, author.
Title: The ancient Chinese / by Elizabeth Andrews
Description: Minneapolis, Minnesota : Pop!, 2023 | Series: Ancient civilizations | Includes online resources and index.
Identifiers: ISBN 9781098243241 (lib. bdg.) | ISBN 9781098243944 (ebook)
Subjects: LCSH: China--History--Juvenile literature. | Chinese--Juvenile literature. | Ancient civilization--Juvenile literature. | Indigenous peoples--Social life and customs--Juvenile literature. | Cultural anthropology--Juvenile literature.
Classification: DDC 972.01--dc23

*Scanning QR codes requires a web-enabled smart device with a QR code reader app and a camera.

TABLE OF CONTENTS

Ancient China can be traced back nearly 50,000 years. At the very beginning, the humans living in China were hunters and gatherers. This meant they traveled around hunting animals and **foraging**.

Around 10,000 BCE, humans settled into villages. They lived around and between two rivers called the Huang He and Yangtze. This land was healthy and good for farming. Slowly the small villages merged into larger kingdoms. Around 2,000 BCE, the original villages had become small states.

The Warring States period began in 475 BCE. Seven states fought for total rule over China. For more than 200 years there was competition. But technology and society were improved by each state working to be the strongest. In 221 BCE, the Qin dynasty united all of China.

People lived on land that was owned and ruled by lords. **Peasants** tended fields and animals. Men farmed grains like rice and millet. Women worked inside making wine, cooking, raising silkworms, and weaving. The rich lived in city centers. These people were court officials, tradesmen, **scholars**, and craftsmen.

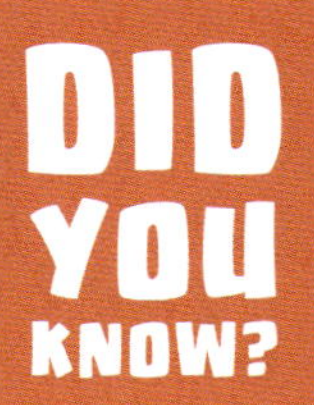

Multiple **generations** of a family lived in one home. Elders were highly respected.

Cities were walled for protection.

People would walk the streets during

market days. They could buy meat, fish,

and vegetables. Clothes made of silk,

cotton, or linen were available. So were

saddles and jewelry.

CHAPTER 2

ANCIENT DYNASTIES

Ancient China's history is divided by dynasties. Dynasties are societies ruled by specific families during a certain period of time. The title of Emperor was passed down from father to son, older brother to younger brother, and one time, husband to wife.

Emperor Kangxi ruled over
China from 1661 to 1722 CE.

In ancient China, scholars were very important. They educated Chinese people.

Dynasties lasted anywhere from ten years to hundreds of years. If a dynasty was successful, it would continue. But when the government failed in any way, **peasants** would **rebel**. The ancient Chinese believed in the Mandate of Heaven. This meant that emperors were chosen by the gods. If emperors did not use their power for good, bad things would happen. Natural disasters or an emperor failing to have a son were bad signs. People believed these were proof from the gods that a dynasty should end.

Some historians believe that the Xia dynasty of 2100 BCE was the first. But its existence has never been proven.

The Shang dynasty held power starting around 1600 BCE until 1040 BCE. It was located in northeast China near the Huang He and Yangtze Rivers. They had their own writing system.

Over the centuries, each new dynasty provided its own **innovations**.

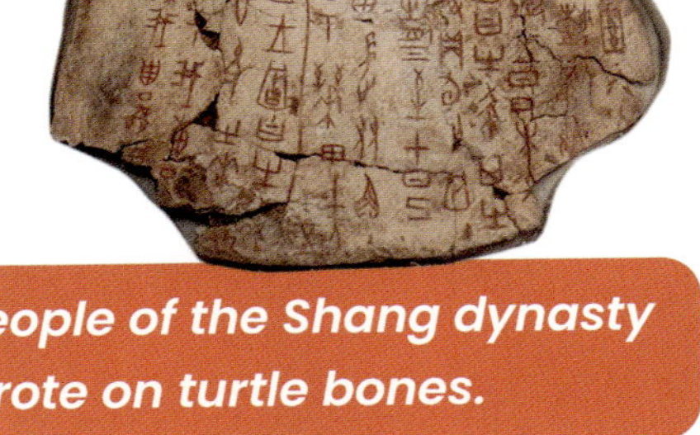

People of the Shang dynasty wrote on turtle bones.

China's boundaries were constantly changing. In 246 BCE, a man named Qin Shi Huang became a new ruler in China. At that time, the land was divided into seven states. By 221 BCE, Qin Shi Huang had conquered all of them and created Imperial China. From then on, a single emperor ruled over all of China.

The famous terra-cotta army was built to guard the Qin ruler during his afterlife.

The Han Dynasty ruled for 400

years starting in 206 BCE. Most Chinese

people living today are related to the

Han people. This dynasty is known for connecting the Silk Road to the Mediterranean Sea. The Han dynasty was also the first to allow regular citizens to have leadership roles in court. The

Song Dynasty was the last to exist in ancient China. It was conquered in 1211 CE by the **Mongols**.

XIA DYNASTY

Researchers have not been able to find clear evidence to prove that the Xia dynasty existed. However, ancient bamboo scrolls mention the dynasty. And a few uncovered historical sites might be one of the capitals of the Xia dynasty. The mystery is still unsolved.

RELIGION AND PHILOSOPHY

The ancient Chinese believed a person had two souls. One soul died when a person's body died. The other soul went to a heavenly place and watched over its living family. People from as early as the Shang dynasty would burn incense and

put out food offerings to their ancestors.

If they didn't give enough respect to their

ancestors, their ghosts may haunt them.

In ancient China, a man named

Confucius lived from 551 to 479 BCE.

He was a leader in **spirituality** and

philosophy. Confucius wanted to

become the best person he could

possibly be. As he gained more and more knowledge, he spread his way of thinking around China. Soon a philosophy called Confucianism guided the Chinese way of life. People wanted to be **morally** perfect. They believed that the good of all people was more important than the good of individuals.

In the 500s BCE, another philosophy called Taoism was started by a teacher named Laozi. This philosophy believed in taking care of the individual over the group. Chinese people who followed Taoism connected to the natural world through meditation, healthy eating, and martial arts.

During the Han dynasty, Buddhism was introduced. It was the first widely practiced religion. Buddhist teachings were like Confucian and Taoist thinking. The goal was to be like the Buddha and reach enlightenment, or a state of total

peace. Chinese Buddhists meditated,

prayed, and did good deeds to reach

this state. The incredible statues and

temples built for worship

still stand in the jungles

and mountains of

China today.

This Buddha statue's hand gesture is for protection and fearlessness.

CHINESE
INNOVATIONS AND ART

The ancient Chinese made some of history's most important inventions. Far earlier than their western neighbors, the Chinese advanced in mathematics, art, trade, and science. Ancient Chinese

people first created things such as the

compass, printing press, crossbows,

and gunpowder.

The first art form used by the

Chinese was pottery. Pottery pieces

dating back more than 30,000 years

have been discovered. Each dynasty improved pottery making. The use of the potter's wheel made sculpting fast. Glazes of different colors gave pieces more elegance and beauty. In 200 CE, the Chinese developed the delicate porcelain they are famous for. It is often called "china."

Chinese astrologers were mapping the stars in 1000 BCE. Their discoveries would lead to the modern clock. Mathematicians from China knew about decimals and negative numbers 1,700 years before the western world.

The world-changing Silk Road was started by the Han dynasty. This was a 4,000-mile (6,437km) trade route. It allowed Chinese traders to share the newest **innovations** with all of Asia,

The complicated silk-making process was kept secret from the world for 2,000 years.

the Middle East, and parts of Europe.

Everyone wanted fancy silks, gems, spices, tea, instruments, and art pieces from the Chinese.

The Chinese made the longest-lasting civilization ever. Their talents and knowledge changed the world.

MAKING CONNECTIONS

TEXT-TO-SELF

Most ancient Chinese followed one of three religious philosophies: Taoism, Confucianism, or Buddhism. Which would you want to follow and why?

TEXT-TO-TEXT

Have you read any other books about ancient civilizations? What did they have in common with the ancient Chinese?

TEXT-TO-WORLD

What are some things that wouldn't exist without ancient Chinese people? How did they change the world?

GLOSSARY

forage — to search for food or supplies.

generation — the period of time between the birth of parents and the birth of their children.

innovation — a new idea, product, or way to do something.

Mongols — people from the Mongol empire north of ancient China.

moral — having to do with what is right and what is wrong in how a person acts.

peasant — farmworkers in Europe and Asia.

philosophy — the study of the meaning of life, truth, knowledge, and other important human ideas.

rebel — to fight against those in control.

scholar — a person who has deeply studied a special field.

spirituality — a meaningful connection to the world and nature beyond oneself.

INDEX

This book is filled with videos, puzzles, games, and more! Scan the QR codes* while you read, or visit the website below to make this book pop.

popbooksonline.com/anc-chinese

*Scanning QR codes requires a web-enabled smart device with a QR code reader app and a camera.